Truly Foul & Cheesy™

Christmas Facts

& Jokes

Published in Great Britain in MMXIX by
Book House, an imprint of
The Salariya Book Company Ltd
25 Marlborough Place, Brighton BN1 1UB
www.salariya.com

ISBN: 978-1-912537-34-1

SCRIBO   BOOK HOUSE   SCRIBBLERS

1 3 5 7 9 8 6 4 2

A CIP catalogue record for this book is available
from the British Library.

Printed and bound in China.
Printed on paper from sustainable sources.

Created and designed by
David Salariya.

Visit
www.salariya.com
for our online catalogue and
free fun stuff.

PAPER FROM

SUSTAINABLE
FORESTS

Author:

John Townsend worked as a
secondary school teacher before
becoming a full-time writer.
He specialises in illuminating and
humorous information books for
all ages.

Artist:

David Antram studied at
Eastbourne College of Art and then
worked in advertising for 15 years
before becoming a full-time artist.
He has illustrated many children's
non-fiction books.

Truly Foul & Cheesy™
& Cheesy™

Christmas

Facts

& Jokes

This Truly Foul & Cheesy
book belongs to:

....

Written by

John Townsend

Illustrated by

David Antram

BOOK HOUSE
a SALARIYA imprint

Introduction

Warning – reading this book might not make you **LOL** (laugh out loud) but it could make you **GOL** (groan out loud), feel sick out loud or **SEL** (scream even louder). If you are reading this in a library by a **SILENCE** sign… get ready to be thrown out!

Disclaimer: The author really hasn't made anything up in this book (apart from some daft verses and jokes). He checked out the foul facts as best he could and even double-checked the fouler bits to make sure – so please don't get too upset if you find out something different or meet a Christmas-ologist, three wise men, a bunch of shepherds or a fairy on top of a tree.

If I had my way, I'd RATify the lot!

official warning

This book is packed with all sorts about many people's favourite time of year. They get all tingly and gooey at the thought of Christmas. You could even say they get very Santa-mental. Others get a bit grumpy. After all, there's lots of gross, revolting, weird and bonkers balderdash when it comes to Christmas. You're about to find out some amazing Christmassy facts, but be warned... there's plenty of foul and cheesy ERGH hiding under the sparkle. Get ready to unwrap a few stinkers!

First up –

Time to get a few cheesy riddles out of the way...

What do angry mice send each other?
Cross-mouse cards.

What do you get when you cross a bell with a skunk?
Jingle smells.

CLANG

What does Tarzan sing at Christmastime? Jungle bells, jungle bells, jungle all the way.

The joy of Christmas

'Tis the season to be jolly
Till you sit down on the holly.
Brushing prickles from your undies
Often takes a month of Sundays.
All the seasonal romance
Gets lost with holly in your pants.
Look away when, on all-fours,
Nan displays her sparkly drawers.
You won't believe what just fell out...
Tinsel, crisps and half a sprout!

9

Advent

Before we dive into the whole squelchy Christmassy mix, don't forget the build-up before the big day. (By the way, did you hear about the chef who was drowned while making a huge Christmas pudding? He fell in the mixture and was dragged under by a very strong currant). The four weeks leading up to Christmas Day are called Advent, which means 'coming'. Although we now associate Advent with calendars and chocolate treats for each day in December, the history of Advent goes back a long way. For Christians, it became the first season in the church year and the time to get ready to celebrate the birth of Jesus. Advent begins four Sundays before Christmas Day.

This is getting far too ADVENTurous for me!

Why is it getting harder to buy Advent calendars? Because their days are numbered.

I can't get to the chocolates in my advent calendar. Foiled again!

What happened to the man who stole an advent calendar? He got 25 days.

Back to basics

(just in case you've come from another planet)

Christmas is now a worldwide annual Christian holiday held on 25th December to celebrate the birth of Jesus. It wasn't always a holiday and only began to become widely celebrated less than 200 years ago. As far back as the fifth century, various feasts took place from 25th December to 5th January (the traditional 12 days of Christmas).

2 If you received all the gifts from the song 'The Twelve Days of Christmas' you would have 364 presents*. The chances are, you wouldn't really want most of them and they'd make a terrible mess of your bedroom. (Apparently the 'Twelve Days of Christmas' came from a belief that it took the wise men 12 days to find baby Jesus, while the words of the song were thought to be codes for Catholics being persecuted long ago.)

*If you can't work how this number is reached, turn to page 116.

3 In Britain, a traditional Christmas dinner once included a pig head served with mustard. Maybe the cook was too pig-headed to serve anything else.

4 It is believed that decorating Christmas trees began in 16th century Germany, when Christians would bring trees indoors, decorated with apples, nuts and dates. In the 18th century, Christmas trees began to be decorated with candles (they didn't worry about health and safety). Electric Christmas tree lights were first used in 1895. It was the royal family (Queen Victoria and her German husband Prince Albert) who made Christmas trees popular in Britain from the 1850s.

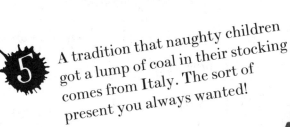

5 A tradition that naughty children got a lump of coal in their stocking comes from Italy. The sort of present you always wanted!

6 Santa Claus is also known as St. Nicholas, Father Christmas, Grandfather Frost and Kris Kringle – or just as daddy in a dressing gown. (More about him later.)

Fairy happy Christmas poem

'I'll tell you something,' said the
fairy, perched up on the tree,
'You'd be surprised what things go
on and what I often see.
On Christmas Eve they left mince
pies for Santa in a pot...
When midnight struck, a mouse
ran in and promptly scoffed the lot.'

'I'll tell you something else,' said
Fairy, perched up on the tree,
'You'd be surprised what things go
on and what I often see.
Last night the cat climbed to the
top and dabbed me with its paws
Then scratched a Father Christmas
toy – a case of Santa CLAWS!'

17

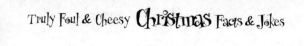

'I'll tell you something else,' said Fairy,
perched up on the tree,
'You'd be surprised what things go on
and what I often see.
On Christmas Eve, when Santa
called, it all got very smelly...
When reindeer stomped into the room
and pooed behind the telly.'

Help - I'm
hidden under bells.
I demand the 'No
bell prize for
Christmastry'.

18

Shocking news

Guess what? We don't actually know when Jesus was born, so 25th December wasn't his actual birthday. The early Christians had many arguments about when to celebrate 'Christ's Mass'. The first recorded date of Christmas being celebrated on 25th December was in the year 336 CE, during the time of the Roman Emperor Constantine (he was the first Christian Roman Emperor). A few years later, Pope Julius I declared that the birth of Jesus would be celebrated on the 25th December. That date was probably chosen because the Winter Solstice (the shortest day of the year) and the ancient pagan Roman midwinter festivals took place around then – so it was a time when people were already in party mood. Any excuse for another feast during those long, dark, cold, spooky nights.

More shock and horror

Christmas is banned! Well, it used to be. Back in 1647, Oliver Cromwell took over running Britain (after having King Charles I's head chopped off). Cromwell was a Puritan who didn't approve of festive celebrations, including mince pies and Christmas puddings, so he banned them. What a bundle of fun he was!

When the next king (Charles II) took charge, Christmas was allowed again, but it never really took off for another 200 years, in Victorian times. When Charles Dickens wrote a story called 'A Christmas Carol' in 1843, Christmas took off like never before. (Maybe Dickens based grumpy Ebenezer Scrooge on Oliver Cromwell!)

Bah humbug. I hate Christmas.

Mince pies –
The shocking truth

At the time of Oliver Cromwell, mince pies and Christmas puddings were filled with meat, rather than dried fruit as they are today. They were first made in an oval shape to represent the manger that Jesus slept in as a baby. Later, rich people liked to show off at their Christmas parties by having mince pies made in different shapes (like stars, hearts and flowers). The fancy shaped pies could often fit together, a bit like a jigsaw. Now they're usually just made in a round shape, dusted with icing sugar and eaten hot or cold.

I like mine pie-ping hot.

5

mince pie jokes to leave
you begging for more...

Knock knock
Who's there?
Arthur.
Arthur who?
Arthur any mince pies left?

Who hides in the
bakery at Christmas?
A mince spy.

3

Did you know that mince pies cost £2.00 in Jamaica and £3.50 in Barbados? Yes, that's the pie rates of the Caribbean.

4

What do you get if you cross a mince pie with an elephant? Either an elephant that sticks to your teeth or a mince pie that never forgets.

Pie-fect

5

Santa went to the doctor with a problem. He said, 'Doctor, I've got a very sore behind after sitting on a hot mince pie. It's now squashed on my bottom and it hurts.' The doctor replied, 'Well, you're in luck because I've got some cream for that!'

Sorting out your mince pie problem is my PIE-ority.

More back to basics...

What do people really know about 'The Nativity'? That's the story told in the Bible of the birth of Jesus. Parents and children in a survey for the Bible Society in 2012 scored like this:

 knew Jesus was born in Bethlehem.

 89% knew Mary put the baby Jesus in a manger (a trough for feeding horses or cattle).

 **77%** knew Herod was king at the time.

 46% knew that shepherds were the first to visit Jesus.

14% knew the wise men (not kings) travelled west following the star to Jerusalem.

How many would you get right?

After the Christmas carol service, a small boy shook the preacher by the hand and said: 'When I grow up, I'm going to give you some money.'
'Well, thank you,' the preacher replied, 'but why?'
'Because my dad says you're the poorest preacher we've ever had.'

What about Santa?

Just what has a jolly fat man with a long white beard and a red suit got to do with Christmas? The idea of Father Christmas going around on Christmas Eve to give children presents only developed over the last 200 years, but the name Santa Claus is short for Saint Nicholas.

Saint Nicholas was a bishop who was born in the third century in what is now Turkey. He was rich but generous and had a reputation for helping the poor and giving secret gifts to them. Because of his kindness, Nicholas was made a saint and his feast day is on 6th December (supposedly when he died).

It wasn't until the nineteenth century that stories of Saint Nicholas became popular again, when writers and artists rediscovered the old legends. In 1823 the famous poem 'A Visit from Saint Nicholas' or 'T'was the Night before Christmas', told of Saint Nicholas with eight reindeer. Over a hundred years later, the reindeer really took off when the well-known song 'Rudolph the Red-nosed Reindeer' was written in 1949.

An urban myth says that Santa's red suit was designed by Coca-Cola. Not true! Long before Coca-Cola, bishops like Saint Nicholas wore red robes. So, with a bit of a makeover, a few whiskers and extra calories, the jolly 'ho ho ho' character was born.

Nicholas

nonsense

limerick

One Christmas, the
famous Saint Nicholas
Wore pants that he
wanted to tickle less.
He solved irritation
With one alteration...
He dropped them, so now
he's Saint Knickerless!

Santa riddles

What do you call Santa's helpers?
Subordinate clauses.

What's the difference between Santa Clause and a knight? One slays the dragon and the other drags on the slay.

How things DRAG ON over Christmas!

Happy Christ-mouse.

Why does Santa come down
the chimney?
Because it soots him.

Why didn't Rudolph go to school?
He was elf taught.

Where does Santa stay when he is
on holiday?
In a ho, ho, hotel!

What's King Wenceslas' favourite pizza?
One that's deep pan, crisp and even.
As in...

'Good King Wenceslas looked out
On the Feast of Stephen,
When the snow lay round about,
Deep and crisp and even.'

For the grisly record: good King Wenceslas was actually a duke, not a king. The Feast of Saint Stephen is the day after Christmas Day. In the year 929 CE, Wenceslas of Bohemia spread Christianity throughout his country. This annoyed his mother and brother who met him at a church door and chopped Wenceslas to pieces. Alas, that put an end to him gathering winter fuel and much else. Family arguments at Christmas are nothing new!

What do you call people who are afraid of Santa Claus? Claustrophobic.

(In fact, claustrophobia is the fear of confined spaces – probably something Santa gets inside all those narrow chimneys. For the record… people who have a real fear of Santa and beards have santaphobia. Some people have a dread of Christmas itself and that's called Christougenniatikophobia. That's enough to give you spelling-phobia, too).

This isn't looking grate.

35

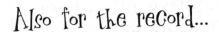

Also for the record...

Shock, horror… Santa's reindeer shouldn't be called Rudolph but Rudolphina. Although both male and female reindeer grow antlers in the summer each year, male reindeer drop their antlers well before Christmas. Female reindeer keep their antlers until after they give birth in the spring. So, if all those images of Santa's reindeer with antlers are to be believed, Rudolph and her friends are all girls.

Yay - Santa's sleigh is driven by girl power!

Wayne Rooney was about to switch on the Christmas lights in the high street. The mayor and his wife stood next to him on the balcony and proudly clapped as the giant switch was unveiled. At that moment, a man in the crowd shouted up, 'Why don't you get a proper celebrity to do the job?'

'How rude,' the mayor's wife gasped. 'We do apologise, Mr Rooney.'

The mayor smiled. 'That's only Alf, the head of the Football Association. So it's all right... Rude Alf, the head, knows Wayne, dear!'

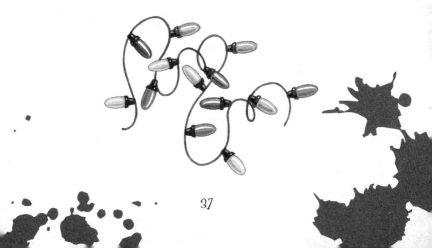

On Christmas Eve, three people stepped into a lift at the Ritz Hotel in London. They were a famous politician who never told a lie, a professional footballer who didn't play for money and Santa Claus. As the lift descended, they each noticed a £50 note lying on the lift's floor. Which one picked up the £50 note and handed it in at reception?

Santa, of course. The other two don't exist!

Did you know that Father Christmas used to be a bus driver? He had to give it up as he couldn't stand people talking behind his back.

Father Christmas: Doctor, I've been so cold on my sleigh and I'm shivering so much I can no longer pronounce my F's, T's and H's. I can only say my name is -A- -ER C-RISMAS.

Doctor: Well, you can't say fairer than that then.

Mistletoe

Did you know that mistletoe is a parasitic plant that grows on various trees? The tradition of hanging it in the house goes back before Christ to the times of the ancient Druids. It was supposed to bring good luck and ward off evil spirits. It was also used as a sign of love and friendship in Norse mythology and that's where the custom of kissing under mistletoe came from.

Kiss someone under here and they'll turn into a frog. They'll be mistle-toad.

Don't let a fool kiss you – or a kiss fool you!

FOUL ALERT: The name mistletoe comes from two Anglo Saxon words – 'mistel' (which means dung) and 'tan' (which means twig or stick). So yes, you're basically bringing into your home 'poo on a stick' and hoping to kiss under it! It is probably called this because mistletoe can be spread from tree to tree in bird droppings. Nice.

Christmas crackers

Christmas crackers were first made in the 1840s by a London sweet maker called Tom Smith. His sweets wrapped in pretty paper with riddles weren't selling too well. Then, while he was sitting in front of his log fire one night, sparks and crackles spat out. Suddenly, he thought what a fun idea it would be if his sweets and toys could be opened with a crack when their fancy wrappers were pulled in half. Before long, his crackers had paper hats inside to look like crowns (as if worn by the Wise Men), as well as cheesy jokes and riddles.

6

riddles from Christmas crackers

Why was Cinderella so bad at football?

She had a pumpkin for a coach and she kept running from the ball in a glass slipper.

Why is it so cold at Christmas?

Because it is Decembrrr.

What beats its chest and swings from Christmas cake to Christmas cake?

Tarzipan.

What do you get if you have a Christmas decoration stuck in your throat?

Tinselitis.

If you laugh at these you must be crackers.

What sort of magic dog makes a good Christmas present?

A Labracadabrador.

What do you call a snowman wearing sunglasses?

A puddle.

Did you know?

The biggest Christmas cracker pull was done by 1,478 people at an event organised by Honda in Japan in 2009. What a cracker!

The world's longest Christmas cracker measured 63.1 metres (207 feet) long and 4 metres (13 feet) in diameter and was made by parents of schoolchildren in Chesham, UK, in 2001.

The longest Christmas cracker pulling chain involved 1,081 people and crackers, achieved by The Harrodian School, London, UK, in 2015.

Very expensive crackers, such as 'Millionaire's Crackers' have contained a solid silver box with gold and silver jewellery inside. The jokes were probably still rubbish!

The most Christmas crackers pulled in one minute by a team of two was 63, achieved in Germany in 2016. That's more than one per second.

Top 10

Cool Christmas jokes from the Foul and Cheesy Christmas party:

1 In the Christmas holidays I went to the zoo and saw a baguette in a cage. I think it must have been bread in captivity.

2 We played Scrabble last Christmas, but all the kids threw the tiles at each other. It was great fun till someone lost an i.

3 We went out for a Christmas meal but instead of turkey, they served us roast pelican. It tasted all right, but the bill was massive.

If you try to eat a pelican, you'd best make sure your belly-can.

48

I asked my sister what she wanted for Christmas. She told me 'Nothing would make me happier than beautiful earrings.' So I bought her nothing.

 What do they sing at a snowman's birthday party? 'Freeze a jolly good fellow...'

 This Christmas I got the perfect present to make the kids' little faces light up when they opened it. It was a fridge.

 When the writer of 'The Hokey Cokey' party song died, it was a struggle getting him in the coffin. They put his left leg in... but that's when all the trouble started.

These jokes are just too fowl and cheesy for me.

8 We were so poor when I was little that we couldn't afford a turkey for Christmas. We gave the budgie a chest expander and hoped for the best.

9 Did you hear about the man who was arrested for stealing Christmas party balloons? The police held him for a while and then let him go.

10 This Christmas we had all the trimmings. That's the joy of being a hairdresser.

Feasting

A big part of Christmas celebrations around the world is the food, but some of the traditional dishes you might not find to your taste. Others might make you dribble with yumminess. Be warned!

Poland

The traditional Christmas Eve supper has 12 non-meat dishes, representing the months of the year and featuring fish such as pike, herring and carp. Other dishes are fish soup, sauerkraut with wild mushrooms or peas and special Polish dumplings. If you don't like fish, it won't just be the mushrooms that are wild!

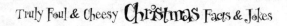

Czech Republic

Traditionally the tree is not lit before Christmas Eve when they have a big dinner of fish soup, salads, eggs and carp. Scarily, the number of people at the table must be even or it is believed the person without a partner will die next year. Quick, get the dog a chair at the table.

Call me a chicken, but I'm petrified of stuffing.

Jamaica

Christmas dinner usually has plenty of rice, chicken, ox tail and curried goat. Or there's Jamaican-style ham studded with pineapple slices, cherries and cloves. A traditional drink at Christmas is made from steeping sorrel petals, ginger and cloves, to make a tasty kind of tea. That's a lot of zingy flavours.

Italy

Christmas dinner in Italy can last for more than 4 hours. Most families will have 7 or more courses including antipasti, a small portion of pasta, a roast meal, followed by 2 salads and 2 sweet puddings – then cheese, fruit, brandy and chocolates. Phew. Then it's time for supper.

Sweden

The Christmas feast consists of caviar, shellfish, cooked and raw fish and cheeses. Then there's a rice pudding – but hiding in the creamy sludge is just one almond. The lucky person who finds the almond will get married within the year. If marriage isn't for you, just give it to the dog.

Almonds are so expensive, they cost an almond a leg.

Greenland

A tradition is to eat fermented birds (food called kiviak) over the winter season for celebrations. Here's the delicious recipe:

1 Collect approximately 400 auks (sea birds).

2 Stuff them – beaks, feathers, feet and all – into the hollowed-out body of a seal.

3 Press out as much air as possible from the carcass and seal it (spot the pun) with seal grease to prevent it rotting too much.

4 Cover the dead seal with a large rock pile for approximately 3-18 months. During this time, the auks ferment inside the seal until they can be eaten – raw!

5 Hold your nose, eat and enjoy. No sprouts necessary.

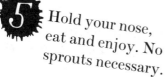

Christmas fowl facts

In many countries, it has become tradition to eat turkey as a great way to celebrate (unless you're a turkey).

Quick turkey facts:

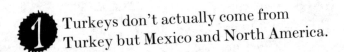

1 Turkeys don't actually come from Turkey but Mexico and North America.

2 Native Americans hunted wild turkey 1,000 years ago. They also used turkey feathers to stabilise arrows and decorate ceremonial dresses.

3 In Charles Dickens' 'A Christmas Carol', Bob Cratchit had a goose before Scrooge bought him an expensive turkey.

4 Turkey meat was a luxury right up until the 1950s, when the birds were reared in huge numbers and became much cheaper. Yes, turkeys going 'cheap cheap'.

Off with its giblets!

5 Henry **VIII** was the first English king to enjoy turkey (as a change to peacock or swan). No doubt he chopped off the head himself! Eating turkey at Christmas didn't become fashionable for commoners for centuries.

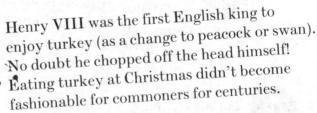

6 Turkeys are believed to have been brought to Britain in 1526.

7 Each Christmas, people in the UK eat about 10 million turkeys (about 76% of families tuck into roast turkey). But there's a downside.

8 Brace yourself… GROSS ALERT. Turkey fat has caused huge Christmas dinner FATBERGS in sewers when people pour all that turkey gunge down the sink into drains. Tons of fatty gunk sets as hard as concrete, causing massive 'fatbergs' which block sewers and cause floods. Water companies warn of blocked drains after all the fat from Christmas roast potatoes, buttered greens, turkeys and sausages. Apparently, enough cooking fat is tipped away each year by UK households to power 110,000 homes with electricity. So just remember… it's better to recycle than tip Christmas down the sink.

Sprouts

Of all the food at Christmas, there's one that can cause quite a stink – the humble Brussels sprout. You either love them or loathe them. So why do some people gag at the taste, while others find them a mouth-watering delight? After all, they're only little cabbagy buds from Pakistan and cultivated in Belgium from around the 13th century. Probably since the 1500s they appeared on Christmas tables, particularly around Brussels.

They nag me to eat my greens but I can't - I'm colour blind.

A serving of sprouts contains four times more vitamin C than an orange, and a cup of cooked Brussels sprouts contains only about 60 calories. So, they're good for you. Convinced? The trouble is, sprouts are often overcooked and boiled too early for Christmas dinner (sometimes it tastes like they've cooked since November). Not only does over-boiling destroy their vitamins, but also makes them smell like rotten eggs.

Foul smells

To put it bluntly, sprouts can give you wind. The problem with sprouts is that they contain chemicals that our bodies struggle to break down. That means they get only partly digested when they move from the stomach through to the colon. Here the bacteria go a bit crazy, trying to work on all that sprouty goo – so sometimes the effects are noisy, smelly or both.

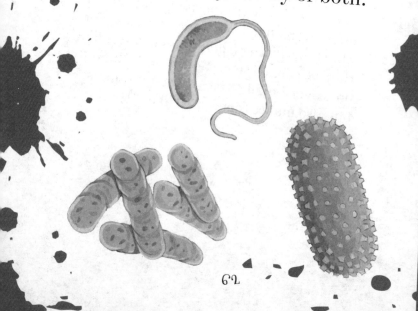

If I tell you about sprouts and indigestion, try not to repeat it.

To put it even more bluntly, sprouts contain sulphur, which protects them from animals wanting to chomp their leaves. This sulphur makes the slightly bitter taste that some people hate and other people love. The bacteria in our bodies turns that sulphur into extra smelly gases, which (brace yourself) can result in distinctive 'sprout farts'. If you hate Brussels sprouts, think of this as a superpower that protects you from sulphur and a windy Boxing Day.

A tasteless limerick

In case you might have any doubts,
At Christmas time or thereabouts,
Of the cause of foul gases
That steam up your glasses...
The culprit is bound to be sprouts!

YUCK!

Did you know?

Science has discovered that children have different taste buds from adults, so sprouts actually do taste much more bitter to a child than an adult. Science also suggests there might be a 'sprout gene' that gives some people more sensitive taste buds. Apparently, more females have such a gene, as 35% of women compared to 10% of men can detect bitter tastes more intensely than the 'average' person who can gobble down sprouts with relish.

Just for the record...

About a quarter of us have a variation of this 'taste gene' (known as TAS2R38), enabling us to identify bitter toxic plant compounds. Scientists say people with the gene can taste the bitter flavour of sprouts about 60 times more strongly. So if you feel sick at the sight, smell and taste of sprouts, just blame your genes.

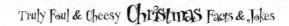

Record breaker

Someone without the 'yucky sprout gene' is Linus Urbanec from Sweden, who holds the world record for the most Brussels sprouts eaten in one minute. He swallowed 31 in 60 seconds in 2008. That's one every two seconds. Please don't try it – just think of the after-effects.

I hope I'm not sitting downwind.

Risky Christmas

Did you know that Christmas is a dangerous time of year? Hospitals can be busy dealing with all kinds of seasonal mishaps. It's all down to elf and safety!

Coming up are common Christmas injuries...

67

Accident & Emergency hospitals often treat injuries on Christmas Day like:

1 Broken arms after cracker pulling accidents.

2 Injuries from out-of-control Scalextric cars

3 Severe injuries from testing batteries on the tongue (never try this).

68

ZAAPP!

4 Electrocution from watering Christmas trees while the fairy lights are plugged in.

5 Tripping over toys and trailing cables to new electrical appliances.

6 Injuries caused by not removing all pins from new shirts.

I don't like Christmas any more!

7 Cuts from knives and scissors used to open presents.

8 Broken parts of plastic toys stuck in the soles of feet.

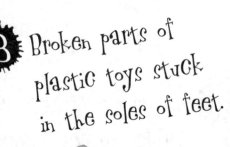

70

9 Children falling off rocking horses or smashing new bikes into walls.

10 Gravy exploding in microwave ovens, hot fat spilled while grappling with a turkey and cuts when chopping piles of vegetables.

Funny gravy accidents make me a laughing stock.

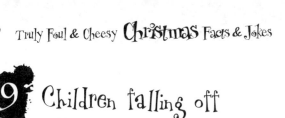

Among the hundreds of people seeking medical help at Christmas in USA:

 An 86-year-old man whose hand seized up after writing too many Christmas cards.

 A 42-year-old woman with a foot injury after 'doing a lot of Christmas shopping' in sandals.

3 A 37-year-old man who developed neck pain after 'a long gift-wrapping session'.

4 A 13-year-old girl with foot pain after 'wearing new shoes that she got for Christmas'.

 5 A 26-year-old man who danced so much at a Christmas party he developed 'severe left ankle and knee pain'.

6 A 49-year-old woman who suffered a bone fracture after falling on her bottom while hanging Christmas lights.

73

Did you know Christmas can be bad for your health?

Scientists and doctors have noticed how more people die at Christmas than at other times of the year. Yes, it seems many people are dying for Christmas – literally.

In places like the **UK** and the **USA**, cold weather and a rise in influenza in December may be a cause. But what about places where Christmas occurs during the summer? Studies have shown that emotional stress, changes in diet and reduced medical care at holiday time may be to blame. Many elderly patients delay seeking medical help over the holiday but then suffer the consequences a few days later.

The final straw was that last cold sprout.

Just a little reminder of horrid Herod, Harold.

It gets worse

Three days after Christmas has a bit of a nasty reputation. 28th December has long been thought of as an unlucky date. In many countries no one would marry or start a new building on that day. An old English custom was to beat children on that date to remind them of the Christmas story when King Herod cruelly killed all the babies in Bethlehem. Luckily this custom seems to have stopped by the 18th century. How about bringing it back?

More silly riddles

Why are horse-drawn Christmas sleighs so useless?

Because horses are rubbish at drawing.

What is the best Christmas present in the world?

A broken drum – you just can't beat it.

What did the Christmas card say to the stamp?

Stick with me and we'll go places.

How did Mary and Joseph know that Jesus was 4 kilograms when he was born?

They had a stable relationship and a weigh in a manger. ('Away in a manger...')

Have an ice day!

Why was the snowman looking through the carrots?

He was picking his nose.

Can you believe it?

Catalonia, a region in northeast Spain, has some 'interesting' Christmas traditions.

GROSS ALERT... They have something called 'the pooping log'. Yes, really. People hollow out a log, then add legs and a face. They 'feed' him every day beginning on December 8th. On Christmas Eve or Christmas Day, they put him in the fireplace and beat him with sticks until he poops out all the small sweets, fruits and nuts. The final things he poops are a salt herring, a garlic bulb, or an onion. Yuck.

But that's not all. Another tradition is a Christmas statue found in nativity scenes. Tucked away behind Mary and Joseph is a strange little man sitting on a toilet! He is called the Caganer but no one seems to know where he came from – even though he's been pooing in the stable for over **200** years.

He must have been put there in loo (in lieu) of an angel.

More fairy business

'I'll tell you something,' said the fairy,
perched up on the tree,
'I see all sorts of things from here
that happen under me.
Last night, beneath the fairy lights,
when all the room was dark,
I watched the dog come running in,
like he was in the park.
He sniffed around the tree trunk and
it wasn't very pleasant
When he raised a leg, gave one
quick yelp and widdled on a present!'

That's what
I think of
Christmas.

Talking of Christmas trees and foul phenomena...

How would you stop people stealing
Christmas trees that are growing on your
land? A council once got so fed up with
people helping themselves to the Christmas
trees in its plantations that they sprayed
the trees with something disgusting that
wouldn't harm the trees – human waste
from a nearby sewage plant. It did the
trick. For some reason, no one fancied
taking home one of the freshly decorated
Christmas trees with its new distinct aroma.

81

6 great books for Christmas – and their authors

1 How to get a Great Present
B Good

2 The Worst Present
M.T. Box

3 Guessing your Presents
P King

4 Christmas Music
Carol Singer

5 The Art of Kissing
Miss L Toe

6 Where's the Gravy?
Sonia Sprouts

Scary Christmas facts and figures for the UK

20 million British shoppers are out buying last minute presents and food on Christmas Eve.

957 – the typical number of calories in the average Christmas dinner, although that number rockets with all those little extras.

6 million – the number of rolls of sticky tape sold in the UK in the run up to Christmas.

1.8 billion Christmas cards are sent each year in the UK alone. 62,824 is the record number of Christmas cards sent by a single person in a year (Werner Erhard of San Francisco in 1975).

600,000 – The number of letters sent to Santa every year.

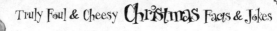

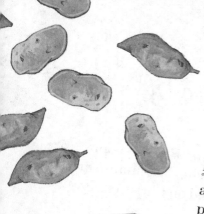

120,000 tons – the weight of potatoes that will be eaten over Christmas.

£48 million – the total amount spent on Christmas puddings in the UK.

230,000 tons – that's the amount of wasted food thrown away each Christmas in the UK, worth around £275 million.

£450 million spent on chocolates every Christmas, followed by 5 million indigestion tablets swallowed to help us all recover from overeating.

2,340,000 miles per hour – the speed that Santa's sleigh would need to travel to reach every home in the world on Christmas Eve (just as well that he has lots of helpers).

£22 billion is spent by UK households at Christmas, with the average household spending £796. Of this, £160 is thought to go on food and drink and the rest on gifts, cards, trees and decorations (Source: YouGov).

Christmas Day is now a busy time for shopping, mainly on smartphones. Over £600 million is spent online on Christmas Day in the UK (over £440,000 per minute).

Online shopping took off back in 1995 when eBay and Amazon began.

85

Christmas verse

'Twas the night before Christmas, when
all through the house
Not a creature was stirring, except
for a mouse...
Which, with only one click, flashed up
'Buy without stopping'...
You can't beat last-minute Internet shopping...
And then, in an instant... a roar
through the night...
Santa delivers – far faster than light!

Five festive fun facts for impressing (or boring) your friends

1 The tradition of putting tangerines in stockings comes from 12th-century French nuns who left socks full of fruit, nuts and tangerines at the houses of the poor.

2 The first commercial Christmas cards were started by Sir Henry Cole in London in 1843. One of his cards sold for £8,469 in 2014.

3 Robins on Christmas cards started about 150 years ago when postmen wore red tunics and were nicknamed Robins.

 If all the Christmas wrapping paper we use is put end to end, it would stretch almost four times around the world.

 Christmas trees usually grow for about 15 years before they're sold. Nearly 60 million Christmas trees are grown each year in Europe.

Silent night

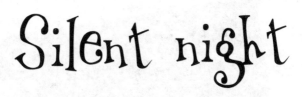

One particular Christmas has gone down in history with its 'peace on earth' message. Sadly, it was all too short and during the tragic events of World War One.

On Christmas Day 1914, rifles firing and shells exploding fell silent along the Western Front, as a sign of goodwill between enemies. Starting on Christmas Eve, many German and British troops sang Christmas carols to each other from their trenches across the lines. At the first light of dawn on Christmas Day, German soldiers emerged from their trenches and approached the British lines, calling out 'Merry Christmas' in English.

British soldiers gingerly climbed out of their trenches and shook hands with the enemy. The men exchanged some of their rations and Christmas puddings and played a friendly game of football in the middle of No man's land.

This so-called Christmas Truce of 1914 came only five months after the outbreak of war in Europe. Although the fighting lasted another four years, such a truce was never repeated, as future attempts at Christmas ceasefires were forbidden. Even so, that Christmas of 1914 was amazing proof that the true spirit of Christmas could break into the darkest of places.

In another 52 years we'll thrash you in the World Cup.

Boxing Day

I find this bit so exciting - as you can see.

The day after Christmas Day (26th December) is celebrated by some as St Stephen's Day, but in a few countries as Boxing Day (UK, Canada, Australia, South Africa and New Zealand). In Germany it is known as 'Zweite Feiertag' (which means 'second celebration').

Boxing Day began in Britain about 800 years ago, during the Middle Ages. It was the day when church collection boxes were opened and the money inside given to poor people.

Much later, the day became a holiday for servants, as one day off from work to celebrate Christmas with their families. 100 years ago, workers such as milkmen, bakers and butchers delivered goods to many houses, and Boxing Day became the day for them to collect their Christmas box or tip.

Today, Boxing Day is a national holiday in many countries, when sporting events are held and when shops start their big sales. Mad stampedes, injuries and sometimes deaths have occurred during Boxing Day sales. It has also become the day to do something wild, like take a plunge in icy seas, lakes and rivers for a fancy-dress swim, often to raise money for charities. And, of course, the day has become associated with eating cold turkey, leftovers and going to the theatre for the start of the pantomime season.

Christmas pantomimes

There's nothing quite like a good panto at Christmas (maybe you think there's no such thing as a good panto at all!). This peculiarly British form of entertainment goes back a long way. So, what's so special (or bonkers) about them? There are rules that most pantos follow:

I'll look totally gorgeous – oh yes I will!

1 The principal boy (the main, young, romantic male character) is played by a woman.

2 An older woman (usually the principal boy's mother) is played by a man who is known as 'the dame' (yes, it's all very confusing).

3 Audience members can be called up on the stage or asked to join in with songs.

4 There's a lot of audience participation, including calls of 'He's behind you!' when the baddie comes on or 'Oh, yes it is!' and 'Oh, no it isn't!' The audience boos and hisses at the villain so it gets very noisy.

5 There's often a pantomime cow, horse or other animal played by people in an animal suit.

6 There's usually plenty of 'slapstick', making lots of mess.

7 The ending is always happy – often with the boy and girl falling in love.

8 The jokes tend to be dreadful, corny, cheesy and sometimes a bit rude.

Our dance on stage was rubbish.

It's like we had two left feet.

And just to show how terrible the jokes can be....

Dame: Ah, Woodcutter – I need some firewood for Christmas.

Woodcutter: Of course – there aren't many chopping days left.

Dame: And I need plenty of mistletoe this Kissmass, I mean Christmas.

Woodcutter: How about some holly berries to add some colour?

Dame: I'm afraid I'm colour blind – they just told me at the opticians.

Woodcutter: Colour blind?

Dame: Yes, it came as a real bolt out of the orange.

Woodcutter: Maybe that explains why your dresses are always… uneasy on the eye.

Dame: I'll have you know, every time I'm down in the dumps, I buy myself a new dress to cheer myself up.

Woodcutter: I always wondered where you got them from.

Dame: Don't you think this dress hugs my figure nicely?

Woodcutter: Sort of – not so much hugs as throttles.

Dame: At least someone paid me a compliment today. They admired my driving.

Woodcutter: Are you sure?

Dame: Yes, they even left a lovely little note on my windscreen. It said: 'Parking Fine'. Wasn't that kind of them?

Woodcutter: I hope it wasn't the wicked wizard.

Dame: He cast a spell when I was driving past.

Woodcutter: What happened?

Dame: I turned into a layby. I was lucky. He's been known to turn people into a prawn cocktail. And that's just for starters.

Woodcutter: Well, at least you managed to get away in time.

Dame: I ran all the way up the hill, you know. I'm so tired. I'm absolutely knickered.

Woodcutter: Knickered?

Dame: Exactly – my breathing is in uncomfortably short pants.

That's really put the PANTS into PANTomime.

Being a pantomime horse each evening is a night-mare.

Last Christmas I got a job as a pantomime horse... but quit while I was a head.

Guess the panto

(Can you work out the names of these popular pantos? Answers below.)

1 The original story for this came from the middle-eastern tales *One Thousand and One Nights*. The UK pantomime version has been performed at Christmas for 200 years, with Widow Twankey as the dame.

2 This is a tale from folklore about a boy who chased the giants out of Wales. In 1819, David Garrick produced this show at Drury Lane Theatre in London, with the first ever 'Principal Boy' played by a female.

This pantomime is based on a true character in London in the late 14th century. Unlike the real person, the panto character finds his fortune with help from his cat, whose ratting abilities bring him lots of money.

 For a while, Great Ormond Street Hospital for sick children received royalties every time this pantomime was performed – about a boy who never grew up.

 This is the most regularly performed pantomime of them all. The villains are women.

 Based on a folk tale and first published in 1697, this is a rags to riches story. The pantomime was first seen in Covent Garden around 1817. It has all the ingredients of a traditional pantomime – a dame, a king, a princess, an ogre – and ends in a marriage.

7 This is about a princess, with a bad and good fairy. It was first performed in Drury Lane in 1806 and is also a ballet often performed at Christmas.

8 This pantomime was performed after the Disney film was released at Christmas in 1937 as the first ever feature-length cartoon. Ever since it has been delighting audiences throughout Britain every Christmas. Clue: short adjectives.

Answers:
1. Aladdin
2. Jack and the Beanstalk
3. Dick Whittington
4. Peter Pan
5. Cinderella
6. Puss in Boots
7. Sleeping Beauty
8. Snow White and the Seven Dwarfs (Grumpy, Happy, Sleepy, Dopey, Bashful, Sneezy and Doc – the only dwarf whose name is not an adjective.)

Comic to tragic

While many people enjoyed the fun of pantomimes on Boxing Day 2004, far more were struck by disaster. A massive earthquake under the Indian Ocean caused a tsunami (a huge wave) that swept across the entire region. The quake was the second strongest ever recorded and the estimated 230,000 deaths made this disaster one of the ten worst of all time.

The death toll in Indonesia alone was about 160,000 people, with another 500,000 people left homeless. About a third of the victims were children. Thailand, Sri Lanka and India were also struck, with the killer waves even reaching 5,000 miles away in South Africa.

Christmas
tongue twisters

to try (10 times quickly) with
your friends

FA LA LA

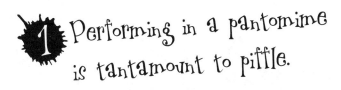 Performing in a pantomime is tantamount to piffle.

2 Seven Santas singing silly songs on snowy sleighs.

3 How many deer would a reindeer reign if a reindeer could reign deer?

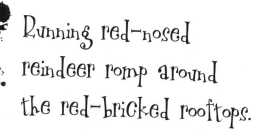 Running red-nosed reindeer romp around the red-bricked rooftops.

I've just lost my teeth in here after saying all those.

5 Santa's snowy sack sags slightly in his sleigh.

6 Santa's swish Swiss wristwatch strap is swiftly switched.

Ring-a-ding-dong

The ringing of bells goes back to pagan winter celebrations. Noisemakers had to clang and clatter to scare away evil spirits in the night. People had fun ringing bells and making a lot of noise. Over time, ringing church bells became important for warnings, celebrations and for bringing people together to make announcements. In Victorian times, it was fashionable to go carol singing with small hand bells to play the tune of the carol. And yes, if it rained… they all got ringing wet!

Christmas Chimes

When bells are unveiled, and
fairy lights trailed
From tinselly corners and crannies,
It's 'kiss-us-time, Christmas-time,
big-sisters-miss-us-time',
Hug aunts, uncles, cousins
and grannies!

When bells begin pealing
or hang from the ceiling,
Entwined with festooned paper chains,
Outside we all stare, wishing
snow everywhere....
Global warming now means it just rains.

With bells ever ringing and
children's choirs singing
Nativity scenes on school stages,
There's Joseph and Mary,
an angel-cum-fairy
And dressing-gowned shepherds and sages.

When bells keep on jingling
and everyone's mingling,
All jovial in the extreme...
The kitchen grows murky
from smouldering turkey,
Gran's specs misting up from
the steam.

If I had my way,
I'd ban Christmas
forever.

DONG!

When bells hang encrusted in dust,
musty, rusted,
Now motionless – silence prevails.
Christmas has gone, and the world
has moved on...
Yippee – it's the JANUARY SALES!

And finally...

The nativity play was going as planned, with Joseph and Mary going from door to door, asking for a room for the night. 'Sorry, we're full up,' came the reply each time.

When they asked at an inn, the innkeeper (played by a small boy in a dressing gown) announced in a loud voice, 'Verily, there is no room in the inn.'

The boy playing Joseph was so startled, he forgot the script. 'Why not?' he demanded. Unperplexed, the innkeeper took a deep breath and boomed, 'You should have booked. We're packed. DON'T YOU KNOW IT'S CHRISTMAS?!'

I've arrived on my new Christmas motorbike. It's a Holly Davidson.

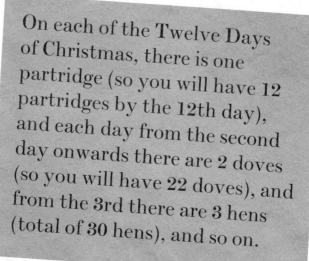

On each of the Twelve Days of Christmas, there is one partridge (so you will have 12 partridges by the 12th day), and each day from the second day onwards there are 2 doves (so you will have 22 doves), and from the 3rd there are 3 hens (total of 30 hens), and so on.

So, how many presents are there altogether?

Partridges: $1 \times 12 = 12$

Doves: $2 \times 11 = 22$

Hens $3 \times 10 = 30$

Calling birds: $4 \times 9 = 36$

Golden rings: $5 \times 8 = 40$

Geese: $6 \times 7 = 42$

Swans: $7 \times 6 = 42$

Maids: $8 \times 5 = 40$

Ladies: $9 \times 4 = 36$

Lords: $10 \times 3 = 30$

Pipers: $11 \times 2 = 22$

Drummers: $12 \times 1 = 12$

Total = 364

If you survived some of the truly foul facts and cheesy jokes in this book, take a look at the other wacky titles in this revolting series. They're all guaranteed to make you groan and squirm like never before. Share them with your friends AT YOUR OWN RISK!

QUIZ

1. Where was Jesus born?

a) Mecca

b) Hollywood

c) Bethlehem

2. Who was the cruel king at the time when Jesus was born?

a) King Harold

b) King Herod

c) King Henry

3. Who was the character of Santa Claus based on?

a) Saint Nicholas in a red robe

b) Joseph in a red cloak

c) Walt Disney in a red sweater

4. Why were mince pies once apparently illegal in Britain at Christmas?

a) They caused deadly food poisoning

b) They were far too expensive

c) They were seen by some as ungodly

5. When did Christmas start becoming popular and commercial?

a) Tudor times

b) Victorian times

c) The 21st Century

6. Who broke the sprout-eating record in 2008?

a) Donald Trump

b) Linus Urbanec

c) Hillary Clinton

7. 12th-century French nuns began the tradition of leaving what in stockings?

a) Frilly knickers

b) Soaps

c) Tangerines

8. What is the day after Christmas Day known as?

a) Saint Stephen's Day

b) Saint Wenceslas' Day

c) Saint Boxers' Day

9. What is a Caganer?

a) A yule log shaped like poo

b) A little man sitting on a toilet in the Nativity Scene

c) A Spanish sausage stuffed with fermented sprouts

10. What did my true love send to me on the 10th day of Christmas?

a) Lords a leaping

b) Maids a milking

c) Pipers piping

GLOSSARY

Catholic a branch of the Christian church with the Pope as its head.

Caviar the salted eggs of sturgeon fish, usually served as a 'luxury' appetiser.

Druid a priest of the ancient Celtic people living in Britain 2000 years ago.

Nativity the time and details of a birth.

Norse mythology ancient stories of Scandinavia, widespread in Germany and Britain until Christianity arrived after the 1st century AD.

Puritan a member of 16th–17th century Protestants who opposed many Church of England customs and preached stricter moral rules.

INDEX

I finished reading this Truly
Foul & Cheesy book on:

........../........../..........